Tales of Victo.

No. 2

The Sheffield Flood

11th March 1864

by
Peter Machan

with illustrations by
Eric Leslie

Alistair Lofthouse DESIGN & PRINT

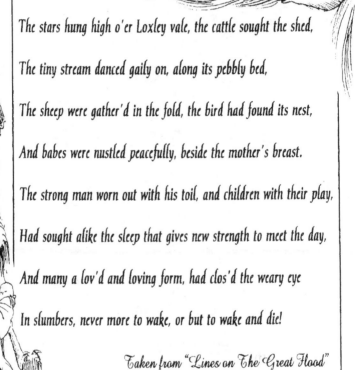

The stars hung high o'er Loxley vale, the cattle sought the shed,

The tiny stream danced gaily on, along its pebbly bed,

The sheep were gather'd in the fold, the bird had found its nest,

And babes were nustled peacefully, beside the mother's breast.

The strong man worn out with his toil, and children with their play,

Had sought alike the sleep that gives new strength to meet the day,

And many a lov'd and loving form, had clos'd the weary eye

In slumbers, never more to wake, or but to wake and die!

Taken from "Lines on The Great Flood"
by L. B. Geoghegan.

1. The Loxley Valley

The River Loxley flows through beautiful countryside in a deep valley, the sides of which are dotted with ancient stone-built farmhouses. Starting its life as a tiny stream in the high, bleak Pennine moorlands, the Loxley soon swells to become a fast-flowing river, before it joins the River Rivelin and then the Don to the north-west of the City of Sheffield. Today the Loxley Valley is a quiet and peaceful place, where people from the city drive out on a Sunday afternoon. In March 1864, however, this tranquil spot was the scene of the worst disaster to hit Victorian England, when the Dale Dyke Dam burst, releasing a wall of water to surge down the sleeping valley, causing destruction on a massive scale.

The Dale Dyke reservoir was the first of a series of five which were planned for the Loxley Valley near the village of Bradfield. Sheffield certainly needed a more reliable supply of fresh water. The population was growing rapidly and the water company could not keep up with the demand. There had been times in recent hot summers when the supply had had to be cut off except for a few hours a week. People often became terribly ill from drinking polluted water and in 1832 there had been a major outbreak of cholera in which four hundred people died. There was no proper sanitation in the town and in summer the mills took so much water out of the rivers that they were reduced to a stinking, slimy trickle.

Even so, it wasn't the poor people of Sheffield who were going to benefit from the 700,000,000 gallons of fresh water stored in the new Dale Dyke reservoir. No, it was the owners of the many mills down the Loxley valley, rolling the steel or forging and grinding the steel tools, who would benefit from the first reservoir, because it was designed to ensure that they had a constant flow of water to turn their wheels. In the tragic event, every one of them would be entirely washed away by the flood.

2. The Dale Dyke Dam is Constructed

Across the Loxley Valley, between the high, bleak Pennine moorlands, about seven miles north-west of the smoky town of Sheffield, an enormous embankment was steadily growing. The work had begun on New Year's Day, 1859, but building the colossal dam wall hadn't been easy. As the navvies dug the foundations, hidden springs of water continually flowed into the excavations and they had to dig deeper and deeper. It wasn't until the great gash had reached a depth of sixty feet that the engineer, Mr. Leather, on one of his few visits to the site from his home in Leeds, agreed with the Sheffield Waterworks resident engineer, Mr. John Gunson, that solid rock had been reached and that building the great wall could now begin.

The first job was to very carefully fill this trench with puddled clay, specially mixed clay and water, to make a waterproof barrier right across the valley. As this wall grew above ground level it was supported on both sides by great embankments of stone and earth which were 500 feet wide at the bottom tapering to 12 feet at the top, 95 feet above the valley floor. Two cast-iron outlet pipes ran through the embankment to the valve house on the outside. The inside of the embankment was faced with closely-fitting stones, but it was the puddle clay core of the wall which was designed to hold back the immense weight of water which the reservoir would hold when filled.

It was now the beginning of March, 1864. The dam wall was finally complete, and the valley which it enclosed had been rapidly filling with water as the previous winter's storms had swollen the streams and brooks draining the moorland basin. Mr. Gunson was a careful man and continually checked to see that everything was in order. In fact, on that Friday afternoon of March 11th, he made the seven mile journey from his house in Division Street, in the centre of Sheffield, to Dale Dyke to settle his anxiety after reading a forecast in his morning paper of unusually heavy rain and gales sweeping in from the west.

By the time Mr. Gunson arrived at the dam the wind was already whipping the water into white-tipped waves and, although he inspected the outer wall, the spray blowing off the dam prevented him from actually walking along the top of the embankment. He saw nothing amiss, however, and after talking to George Swinden, the contractor, he felt reassured that progress on the final touches to the stonework was well in hand, and left to drive himself back down the Loxley Valley, through Hillsborough and on to Sheffield, in the gathering gloom of the stormy evening, at about 5.30pm.

3. The Danger Becomes Apparent

It was at about the same time that Mr. Gunson left that the workmen, who were busy fitting the last of the stone blocks to the far end of the wall, decided to call it a day. William Horsefield usually walked home across the embankment top but today he decided to walk along the outer side of the bank where it was more sheltered from the wind and spray. About half way along he happened to look down, as he pulled his heavy coat around him, and was surprised to see a crack running along the bank, not very wide, but about 50 feet long. He was concerned enough to mention what he had seen to Samuel Hammerton, a local farmer who was making his way in the opposite direction. Mr. Hammerton was more concerned. There had always been local people who were apprehensive about the safety of the enormous embankment after they had seen the difficulties digging the foundations, and now Samuel Hammerton wasted no time in going to George Swinden's house to let him know what he had seen.

By about 7 o'clock a group of about twenty local people could be seen examining the crack by the light of flickering lanterns. "What do you think is the cause of this crack?" asked Joseph Ibbotson, the miller from nearby Lower Bradfield. "This is just a crack caused by the inner part of the embankment settling a little. It is all quite usual" replied George Swinden.

"Then you think there is no danger?" "None whatsoever." But the villagers were by no means satisfied by the reassurances of the contractors and decided to send young Stevenson Fountain into Sheffield to fetch Mr. Gunson.

Meanwhile, the group from Low Bradfield, including Joseph Ibbotson, hurried the mile or so back home to make preparations in case the worst happened. Joseph's brother, William, was particularly agitated as he repeated to the party of neighbours the strange dream that his wife had had the previous night. "She woke with a real fright, I can tell you" he said. "Oh William, she sobbed to me, I dreamt I were drowned. I were trying to get across this narrow bridge and there were water all round. I thought I were done for but just as water was going to wash me away I woke up!" "I can tell you I'm not for me bed tonight." The neighbours agreed that this was indeed a strange coincidence and, making their way to their own houses and cottages, wished each other a safe night. Most of them decided to sit up in front of their fire, fully dressed, just in case.

Young Stevenson had ridden a couple of miles down the valley, to the small group of farms, mills and cottages called Dam Flask, when he almost came to grief. The saddle suddenly slipped, he was thrown to one side and only just managed to pull the horse up safely. The saddle girth had broken and he would be unable to ride any further until it was repaired. He led the horse to the Barrel Inn and went inside to ask for help. While he told the landlord, Johnathan Ibbotson, the reason for his errand, other ears in the small bar listened eagerly. Drinks were hastily drained and the customers left to pass word around of the danger and to make preparations. This was as far as a warning got, for hundreds of people living down the valley the first hint of the disaster would be the tremendous roaring noise moments before the flood struck.

Jonathan Ibbotson quickly provided Stevenson with a new saddle girth and the lad sped on his way. Even so it was nearly an hour later when he brought the horse to a stop outside No. 14 Division Street and knocked on the door. The servant who answered the door did not ask him in but went to fetch Mr. Gunson, who was just finishing his supper. The engineer came quickly and, seeing Stevenson on his own doorstep, was immediately aware of how urgent the men considered the situation to be and, although his wife, Charlotte, tried to persuade him not to go out again on such a wild night, he was already pulling a heavy cloak and hat from the hall stand. "Don't wait up for me, my dear, I may well take lodgings in Bradfield tonight. Don't worry, I'm sure there will be nothing to worry about." His horse was harnessed to the carriage once more, he sent for Mr. Craven, another contractor, and together they set off to make the long journey back through the gas-lit streets, past the tall smoky chimneys of the cutlery and steel works, over the bridge at Hillsbrough and up the Loxley valley. All was quiet and the lights of the town were left

behind. At Malin Bridge the farm dogs barked as the gig sped past and the light streaming from the windows of the Malin Bridge Inn and the sounds of merry Friday night laughter, made the travellers wish that they had time to stop for a while. But hurry as they did, it was ten o'clock before the engineers saw the dark mass of the Dale Dyke embankment rearing up before them.

George Swinden met them and there was quite a crowd of local people, all eager to show Mr. Gunson the cause for their concern. "I'm sorry they've had to send for you, Mr. Gunson. I really don't think it's anything that we can't handle." said Mr. Swinden, leading the way with his lantern. "I dare say you're right. Have you been able to lower the water level yet?" "Yes, we managed to open the release valves, although the pressure was so great that it took almost an hour. They are fully open now but it's going to be some time before we see much effect." They stood peering down at the crack. "Is it the same as when you saw it earlier?" asked Gunson. "No, it's getting wider. See, I can put my whole hand down it now." "This could be a very serious situation. We must relieve the pressure on the wall. Get men to take dynamite and blow a hole in the by-wash weir so that we can get the level down as quickly as we can." A group of workmen were instructed but in the darkness and the blustery weather they couldn't get the fuse to light. Again and again they tried, but to no avail.

Mr. Gunson, however, began to feel that everything would be alright. The water was rushing through the outlet pipes and the pressure on the dam would soon be lower, although it was emptying painfully slowly, and the waves were still breaking over the top of the wall. They would be able to inspect the embankment more closely in the light tomorrow.

He returned to the crack, and looking up, to his horror, saw a white sheet of water flowing over the dam wall and dropping down the crack at his feet. He rushed to the valve house to see if there was any way of hurrying the emptying of the dam but suddenly heard frantic shouts of warning. He only had time to scramble to safety as a great portion of the top of the embankment slid away and millions of gallons of water came roaring through.

4. The Midnight Flood

The water did not just *flow* from the broken dam. Because so much of the wall had collapsed instantaneously it took only a short time to almost empty, which meant that the great wall of water which was now released *tore* down the valley with colossal power, ripping up trees, gouging out the river bed, carrying along sixty ton boulders and smashing buildings and bridges as if they had never stood.

The wall of water pounded down the valley towards the village of Low Bradfield, smashing farmhouses in its wake but, as yet, causing no injuries, all the occupants having been at the dam. The farm dogs gave the first warning that something was amiss, and the Ibbotsons, amongst other villagers were quickly out and spreading the alarm. Mr. Nichols, the village schoolteacher, and his wife watched dumbstruck as the school and nearby chapel were carried away, and all Joseph Ibbotson's worst fears were confirmed as his sturdy, stone-built corn mill shuddered and swayed before subsiding into the foaming waves.

In the bottom cottage of a row near the river lived Joseph Dawson, the village tailor, who had also been up at Dale Dyke earlier. This should have been a happy day for him and his wife as their new baby had been born only the day before. But now they were in terrible danger. Water was surging all round the house and Joseph's wife was still confined to bed with the baby. He decided to take action and, wrapping them both in a blanket he carried them down the stairs and out of the door. Just at this point he looked up to see a great wave bearing down on them. "Turn back!" screamed his wife, "Turn back, Joseph or we'll all be killed!" But it was too late. The water hit them and there was a struggle in which the poor little baby was carried away. The flood's first victim was only one day old. The distraught couple made it back upstairs and were finally rescued by neighbours using a ladder as a bridge between the hillside and the window.

The flood raced on, shattering more mills and farmhouses, before roaring through the village of Dam Flask. Most of the villagers were prepared, having heeded Stevenson's warning, but one of the navvies, with the nick name of Sheffield Harry, refused to believe that such a disaster was possible. He lodged with a couple called Kirk, in a cottage near the Barrel Inn, and when the flood came Mrs. Kirk only just escaped with her cat and dog as the pounding water carried away the cottages, the pub, the mill, the bridge and Sheffield Harry, who was still pulling on his socks.

Four workers were still hard at work at the nearby wire mill, drawing out the wire to make the frames for ladies' crinoline dresses. They were aware of nothing until the end wall of the mill

was torn away and they were all washed to their deaths. It was a similar story at Loxley Old Wheel, where 14 year old Joseph Denton and his 11 year old brother John were still working. There was no warning before the freezing water tore open the door and flooded into the mill. Both boys were thrown into the water, but John managed to climb a pole onto a roof beam, to which he clung, shouting in vain for his brother. In the morning people would express amazement at the sight of a complete haystack standing intact in the middle of the dam. At Rowell Bridge, a little further on, the grinding wheel, which provided work for at least thirty men, was carried away and with it William Bradbury, who had been at work at this late hour. His body would never be identified. At Harrison's Tilt, at Low Matlock, workers Walter Booth and Joe Gregory disappeared in the rushing torrent.

By this time the flood carried along all sorts of debris, smashed furniture, trees, bits of machinery and bodies, both human and animal. It now struck into the Olive Paper Mills, and began to unroll the huge rolls of paper down the valley. Next the wave tore a great hole through the centre of Daniel Chapman's house, carrying off all six occupants, who were asleep in their beds.

But the night's real horror was only just beginning. The village of Malin Bridge stands at the point where the river Loxley joins the Rivelin, right in the flood's path, and so the village took the full force of the torrent, and the settlement was almost wiped out. The first to go was the substantial farmhouse of the Tricket family. The house was unusually full that evening. Mrs. Tricket had attended her mother's funeral only the day before and her father had come to stay with them, and Joseph Barker, who was going to start work at the nearby Limerick Wheel, had come to lodge with the family the same day. Together with their three children and three servants there were ten people in the house, all of whom were swept to their deaths. Next for destruction were both of the pubs, the Stag, where twelve of the Armitage family, including Eliza Armitage, the landlady, and her sons William and Greaves, who were both anvil makers at Mousehole Forge, died, as well as three lodgers, and the Malin Bridge Inn, where five of the Bisby family perished. Near the Tricket's farm stood a row of cottages where only two of the thirteen inhabitants survived. It took little more than ten minutes for the flood to pass, and in that time over ninety people had lost their lives and fifty houses had been destroyed.

And still the flood carried on, now sweeping towards Hillsbrough. In a cottage next to Hill Bridge Henry Whittles somehow managed to cling onto a bed and stop it from being swept through the smashed bedroom wall, as his terrified family huddled on it, forced to watch bodies being swept past in the black, stinking water, and at nearby Brick Row Joseph Hides had the fright of his life when he got up to investigate the loud noise and found that his stairs had been swept away. Quickly he wrenched the leg off a piece

of furniture and used it to smash a hole through the ceiling and make his way along the roof space into the next house.

At the army barracks the family of Paymaster-Sergeant Foulds, newly posted to Sheffield, couldn't begin to understand what was happening as the high boundary wall came crashing down and water started pouring in through the window. "Good God! The world's breaking up! We're all going to drown like rats in a hole!" screamed his wife, but the sergeant managed to smash open the door with a shovel and wade out with his wife and baby. However, when he turned back to rescue his two children the force of water held the door tightly shut, the room filled to the ceiling, and his children were drowned. The flood now swept on through Owlerton and, at the point where the Loxley meets the Don, this great wall of water turned and sped down towards the thousands of people fast asleep in their beds in the crowded streets and alleyways of Sheffield.

It was the poorest people, who lived in the flimsiest dwellings, who would bear the brunt of the disaster. The flood was bearing down on Neepsend, where a large area between the river and the railway embankment, was laid out with gardens and allotments. A surprisingly high number of families lived here, in what were little better than garden huts, along with their chickens, rabbits and their pig. There was little that anyone could do to save these people from the onslaught, as their poor homes were overwhelmed. Thomas

Elston and his family were drowned, the Jetty family were all carried away and when a wave washed all five of the Midwood family into the river only the son, Joel, saved himself by clinging onto a floating piece of furniture. The scene was chaotic. On one side James Wilson was struggling to keep hold of a chimney which he had been washed up against, and nearby Mrs. Bennet clung, screaming, onto a swaying cherry tree until it broke and she was thrown to her death. The three children of the Coggan family perished all alone as water rushed into the cellar in which they slept. Their parents were in Wakefield attending a funeral. John Gannon, a labourer who lived in a small whitewashed cottage, managed to get his wife and six children through the ceiling, out of the house and onto the roof where they were seen sitting, terrified and freezing, as the water tore away at the poorly-built property. There was one last scream, and the house seemed to lift up before disintegrating into the swirling tide, taking all the family down with it.

Fortunately there were also stories of heroic rescues from the swirling flood water. A little way below Neepsend the river was divided into two channels to supply water to the mills. This created a large island in the river, on which a number of people lived, called Bacon Island. The shuttlehouse stood at the head of the island, and James Sharman, the shuttleman, was responsible for opening and closing the shuttle gates to control the flow of water to the wheels. As the flood approached all the Sharman family were sleeping soundly but were soon aroused by the local constable, P.C. Thorpe, hammering on the door. The lower rooms were already flooding as the family looked from the bedroom window. The policeman shouted for Sharman to throw the children into his arms, which he did, one by one, and he managed to carry all seven of them to safety before their parents followed, in the brink of time, as the house was swept away. P.C. Thorpe was later to receive a medal for bravery for his actions that night. A neighbouring cottage, occupied by Mr. Greaves, a treacle boiler, was struck with such force that the stable wall smashed through the wall of the next house and drowned the donkey.

The water now flowed down the narrow streets of red brick terraced houses, extinguishing the street lamps as it went, and rushing down the passageways into the back yards, cutting off the exit of all those who lived there. There were many factories in this poor part of Sheffield, and great damage was being done to these. The water hissed and steamed as it flooded red hot steel furnaces, which exploded as the cold water turned to clouds of white steam. Tall slender factory chimneys toppled and fell, and the stinking contents of the tanning pits at the two tanneries were emptied into the flowing tide. Fifteen year old Edward Cross, who worked at Mills's tannery was the only member of his family to survive after the front wall of their cottage was knocked out. He survived by taking refuge up inside the chimney and staying there until the water level went down.

Many people in this overcrowded district kept a pig in a sty in the back yard, which they lovingly tended and fed throughout the summer so that it would be good and fat and provide food for the family for the winter. At the end of Kelham Island stood three small cottages, in one of which lived John Eaton. He heard the terrible noise of the flood approaching and, looking out of his bedroom window, saw the water approaching. His immediate thought was to save his pig so he rushed down into the yard to try to get the pig out of its house. The pig, however, would have none of it. Try as he did he couldn't coax it, pull it, push it or kick it out. Eaton's neighbours were leaning out of their windows shouting for him to leave the pig and save himself when the wave stuck, tearing down the sty, carrying off the pig and dashing Eaton to his death against a wall. His wife gave one great cry as she rushed down to save him, before she too was swept off her feet and carried far down the river to her death. Dozens of carcasses of pigs, horses and cattle were now being swept along or were washed up in grim heaps behind walls.

In a small cottage near the river in this area, one family experienced an extraordinary escape. Mr. and Mrs. Wells had gone away into the country to collect watercress, which they sold for a penny a bunch in the market in Sheffield on Saturdays. They had left their two children, a boy aged thirteen and a three year old girl, all alone. It was about one o'clock when Mrs. Wells returned and, seeing the whole area completely submerged, immediately thought that her children must have been drowned. When the water went down enough for her to wade through the slimy mud to reach her house she shouted for the children but there was no answer. Eventually she pushed open the door and, since all was quiet, feared the worse. Looking up into the corner, however, she spotted, on the top shelf of the cupboard, the two children, still fast asleep, but quite safe.

The conditions in which some poor people lived were quite astonishingly primitive. In nearby Orchard Lane, Mrs. Crump and her son were drowned in their one room hovel in the yard of the Hope and Anchor, Mrs. Green, a mangelwoman occupying similar accommodation in the same yard, met with the same fate and Dennis Mc'Laughlin drowned next to his donkey, with whom he shared a stable. 'Old Dickie' Hazlehurst earned his living by selling coal and he lived in the shed which doubled as his coal store in a yard in Joiner Lane, sleeping on a box in the corner of the shed. Although he managed to get out when the flood struck, and was heard to scream for assistance, he was washed away and killed, and similarly a man called Peacock, who slept in one of the coal offices at the Midland Station, was drowned there. Nearby young Sidney Varney met his death in a strange way, as he was riding home. He found suddenly that his horse was wading along a flooded street.

All of a sudden a large piece of timber, which was being carried along, hit the horse, causing it to stumble and throw the rider over its head, to his death.

By the time the flood had reached Lady's Bridge, near the town centre, news had spread and quite a large crowd of spectators were running down to see the spectacle. As many as could huddled onto the bridge itself to experience the full thrill of the flood water surging through the arches below them and to see the great piles of debris which were being washed up against it. If they had realised that most of the bridges further up the river had already collapsed perhaps they would not have stood there! In the event, the ancient bridge stood firm, and the crowd of spectators amused themselves by knocking the rats, which climbed up the debris, back into the swirling water.

Beyond the Wicker the valley of the Don broadens out and the flood waters began to spread and to lose some of their tremendous destructive power. The rising water level, however did enormous damage to the great steel works which lined the river and the canal towards Rotherham. The flood claimed its last victim, Thomas Gill, the night watchman, at Hornby's chemical works on Brightside Lane. The great rolling wave of water carried on, churning along with it boilers, beams, carts, beds, chests, pigs and bodies, many of them not coming to rest until the flood finally spent itself, at Doncaster. Nearly two hundred and forty people had lost their lives during this dreadful night. It was to go down in the records as Britain's worst dam burst disaster and the greatest disaster of Victorian England.

Ruins of Malin Bridge Inn

Ruins of Malin Bridge Inn and adjoining houses

Ruins of Waterloo Houses

Ruins of Wisewood Works

5. The Days After the Flood

As daylight dawned on Saturday 12th March, the full scale of the terrible catastrophe began to emerge. In the town the newsboys shouted down the streets with fresh piles of the *Sheffield Daily Telegraph* and *The Independent,* which had printed news of the disaster as reports came in throughout the night. They could have been sold six times over.

"Never has a day dawned on a more complete wreck than are the lower parts of the town this morning" reported the paper.

For hundreds of people who had lost family or most of their belongings, the morning brought terrible sadness. Many people had just wandered about all night in a dazed condition. The Chief Constable, John Jackson, called on the Mayor, Mr. Thomas Jessop, in the early morning, and the two of them set out to see for themselves the damage caused. They were shocked to see the enormous scale of the destruction to their town. As they picked their way along the sludgy streets they saw lamp-posts which had been bent double by the force of the flood, ruined houses and factories, terrible scenes of corpses of animals and people and the appalling distress of those who had lost loved ones and everything

they owned. Right across the busy street at Shalesmoor lay a great piece of timber weighing many tons. They witnessed scenes of people digging bodies and belongings from the piles of waste and mud.

The bodies were placed on carts and taken to local schools, public houses or the Workhouse, where their distressed relatives could identify them. In many cases there was no-one left in a family, and many bodies were never identified. The coroner, John

Webster, had posters printed with descriptions of the bodies to try to get people to identify them, and grieving family members put notices in the newspapers with descriptions of missing relatives. It took some people, such as John Appleton, who toured Rotherham, Kilnhurst, Mexborough and Doncaster, weeks before they found dead relatives, and the last body to be claimed was that of Jonathan Ibbotson, who was finally identified on May 5th. The unidentified bodies were buried in separate graves in the General Cemetery on Cemetery Road.

There was a great danger of disease from the filth and bodies of animals but the Mayor ordered that the streets should be treated with quicklime and fortunately there was no outbreak of sickness.

For miles along the banks of the River Don people had now gone down to the riverside and were poking with sticks to retrieve items which had been washed down. Unfortunately many of these people were not honest and before the day was over the Mayor had to instruct two companies of soldiers from the barracks to stand guard on wrecked houses to prevent looting. Outside the Price's house at Malin Bridge, a valuable gold watch, which had belonged to Charles Price, was found and was handed to his relations, but at the nearby Hillsbrough National School, where some of the dead had been brought, there was such a scramble to get a view of the unfortunate victims through the window that Alderman Gledrill,

who had come from Salford, and Mr. Hughes, from Manchester, had their watches stolen from their pockets. There are still a few sad relics at Sheffield City Museum, which were said to have been washed down by the flood.

The news had quickly spread throughout the whole country and soon hundreds of people were flocking to Sheffield in special excursion trains to see for themselves the site of 'The Great Innundation' and many local people made money by taking them up the Loxley Valley by donkey cart.

Many of them wished to record their visit and so photographers from Sheffield and Manchester were there to take advantage of the trade and sell pictures of the ruins. It was the first disaster to be recorded in photographs, and hundreds of them survive today. There were also rogues who pretended to have been made homeless by the flood and begged money from the great crowds of visitors. One man was said to have made £12 a day in this way, an enormous amount of money at the time.

Queen Victoria took a close interest in the event and sent a personal donation of £200 towards the Relief Fund which had been set up by the mayor. Other towns also sent contributions of money and in two months a sum of £50,000 had been raised. Legally, however, it was the Water Company which was responsible for claims for damage and loss, and so the company quickly raised £400,000 and a committee of commissioners was appointed to investigate all claims for damages.

The Innundation Commissioners had an extremely difficult job in sorting out all the 7300 claims fairly. There were workmen claiming money to replace their tools, families wanting to replace destroyed furniture and widows claiming for their husband's loss of earnings. Some claims were either silly or dishonest. A man, who lived on the Wicker, who said that he earned his living by composing poetry, claimed, and was granted, money to compensate for the loss of his life's work, whilst another claim, which was dismissed, was made by a rat-catcher to compensate him for loss of earnings after so many rats had been drowned!

The inquest, which opened on March 23rd, was a very bad tempered affair, in which emotions were running understandably high. The coroner, John Webster, cross-examined Mr. Leather, the architect, and Mr. Gunson extremely aggressively. His questions constantly implied that he did not consider that the dam wall had not been built with sufficient care. The final verdict of the jury was to haunt John Gunson for the rest of his life:

"There has not been that engineering skill and that attention to the construction of the works that their importance demanded"

A little later a team of experienced engineers did a thorough investigation to find the cause of the collapse. They could not find anything wrong with the way that it had been built. The dam wall was rebuilt a little way up the valley. The water mills were quickly rebuilt and life gradually returned to the stricken Loxley Valley.

Today there are hardly any signs that the terrible flood ever took place.